SOULSKIN
RETRIEVER

………………..(insert your name)…………………

Healing HER II
Copyright © Sez Kristiansen
All rights reserved

Illustrations by Sez Kristiansen

Books can be made available for quantity
discounts in bulk purchases for educational,
business or sales promotional uses.

Other poetry books by Sez

Healing HER Vol.1 (2019)
Story Medicine (2020)
Whole In The Body (2021)

coming soon…
Seekless Meditations

For more information and requests:
www.sezkristiansen.com
hello@sezkristiansen.com

To us.

CONTENTS

INTRODUCTION

Surrender
/sər'en.dər/
the sacred act of collaboration

There is no wiser healer than Surrender.

We are, however, very weary of giving ourselves away to anything that can't offer us a sense of certainty in return. We refuse to let go, even of things that deeply hurt us. We have become war maidens of control and see Surrender as an enemy against our right to self-govern.

There is a heavy stigma attached to the word. We believe Surrender assumes that while we are down and out in life's trenches, rather than whetting our swords, we are bleaching our flags. Surrender seems to be what we are forced to do internally, only after we've first thrown our will at everything outside of us.

If only we could grant ourselves full control over how fast and how well we heal, then we would have no need Surrender and her entourage of self-abandoning qualities. *Or so we think...*

Those of us who have found ourselves with little control over what's happening to us (and most often within us) have come to intimately understand that we *do* hold power even in our darkest moments, but it is not the commanding power we first assumed. It's a choice we must make, a life-altering, palm-splitting choice to either keep holding on or to let go.

Hold on, or let go. Be that of a dream, a person, an identity, a trauma response, or even a healing that's no longer working for us. It is the greatest autonomy we have over our destiny (and probably the only one). And it's not *what* we let go of, but how we allow ourselves to break free from that incessant need to fix ourselves that matters. This is how true healing then happens. And that is why Surrender is a conscious act of collaboration with what is always working *with* us. It's when we finally decide to let go of our resistance against what will naturally rebalance, regenerate and renew us.

When we are brave enough to let go, we often find that what we release from our tightly clenched fists is not what matters most. We never let go of love but of the fear that separates us from our unity with Her, the Divine Feminine. That is because Surrender always returns us to a kind of wholeness, a felt sense that we are not alone in our healing. The act of fully surrendering our smallness to something of much greater capacity shows us how tenderly we have been swaddled by the fabric of the Divine all this time.

Left to the controlling parts of us, healing can feel like we've been tasked with the meticulous and lonely job of weeding a meadow. It's relentless work. However, if we surrendered to the seasons, to the wind, the soil, to the space-holding aspects of our psyches, we would naturally rewild and therefore return ourselves to an innate balance.
Our sole task in life would then be to bloom. And enrich ourselves with that which consistently falls away from us.

We live in an energetically masculine culture, a *do-*
ing culture, a fixing, a compartmentalizing, and
therefore a lopsided culture. We need to learn how
to lean our body weight far over towards the
feminine to balance out what has been burdening
the scale for so long.

Surrender is our devoted teacher. She is our
alchemist. She is infinite intelligence. And yes, She
is a She, She is Her. She is a bending towards the
light. A kneeling upon the earth. A cradling of the
moon. She is a sacred part of the whole, the
Divine Feminine energy within every one of us,
no matter our biology or identification. She shows
us when to howl, when to show teeth and when to
go underground. She is always pregnant with new
life. She is both decomposition and growth so
holds immense wisdom for us in times of personal
transformation. There is good reason why
mythological goddesses representing birth are also
the Valkyries of war.

In our deepest suffering, we have been with Her.
She spoke to us through Grace. She is not absent
of light but darkness herself. She is the winter we

need when we refuse to rest, the midnight guard, the lava-rich soil, the night nurse.

It's a paradox to want to heal ourselves with the masculine part of us that needs healing, but that's the fog of pain we are all in. We cannot rightly see in our depressions that we are using a wounded part of ourselves to try and fix what feels broken, especially when trauma changes how we see the world and ourselves. That is why we so often find ourselves stuck in this never-ending self-healing cycle.

To heal, we must go beyond the mind, beyond who we think we are, and towards a Love that can hold and heal it all. This great capacity comes to us in many surprising forms, from belly-deep laughter to cold water, from forest floors to paint brushes, from good therapists to good listeners. It comes through us from anything that allows us to be who we truly are, and more oftentimes, who we once were long ago.

Many of us do not know the kind of mothering it takes to tend to our deepest wounds while celebrating every piece of our wild selves. Our authenticity has been largely managed to fit the wounded needs of others, and it is to the detriment of our souls. Those of us who have been traumatized do not know what it feels like to embody the gift that *we are* to this world. We are people made of gold who relentlessly seek our preciousness outside of ourselves, and that makes us more disempowered than ever before.

We know the cost of leaning too far into reactive action, impatience, and defense, and it's not because it hasn't taken us anywhere - but because it has taken us to many dis-serving places very fast. We know this intimately because the instability of our world mirrors the imbalances of our bodies.

The part of Surrender we get most wrong is that we believe it should be gentle and soft because it is a Feminine quality. But primordial, source-filled Surrender can be deeply uncomfortable at times, especially before the cellular level of embodiment occurs. When you offer your heartache to Her, she may not always give you light in return. Many of us get impatient with the process of rebirth. We have certain expectations of bloom and lightness but She has her own way of guiding us back to ourselves and knows that it's only through black, nutrient-rich soil that we rise, rooted.

I believe Surrender is the word we used to describe the intuitive way we once lived. In our modern personal and cultural disconnection, we no longer live by Surrender because we feel we have far too much control over far too much choice, and that means almost everything we come into contact with disconnects us from a unifying kind of trust. But what if we returned to that more intimate way of living? What if it was our *only* way of healing? Our control would then be but a small helm in life's great winds, and not the driver of the seasons, stars, and oceans as we currently believe.

The great Her, life bearer, moon eater, asks us to ebb and flow with her through Surrender, for we are but a tide to her pull. Wanting to *be* the moon is how we hurt. It's how we've always hurt. It takes knowing that we are fully responsible but not fully in control of what happens to us. And in practicing that truth every day, we arc ourselves back into the greater circle of wholeness.

You do not need to know everything about healing, just know that you are being supported. The Divine has no greater wish than to meet you half way but She cannot if you insist on doing it alone. So Surrender. Offer yourself to the Her within you, to the many facets of her fierce tenderness, knowing that how you feel right now, in your ache, in your loneliness and disconnect is Her squeezing herself into the world. She is stretching you so there's more of you that can hold space and more of you that can take up space in this world.

Another person is reading this book with you right now, dear friend. And my own healing stains these pages. We are connected through a journey very few are brave enough to take. Remember your courage, always. And may these poems provide you with what only poetry can, *a remedy for the soul.*

BEHIND EVERY FEAR
is the belief that
you are not capable,

that you won't be able
to hold that loss,

that you won't be able
to embody that dream,

that you won't be able
to break free
when you need to,

and even
that you won't
be able to handle that love,
that opportunity, that joy...

but here you are.

After everything,
you're still here.

It doesn't matter

what you face,
what you lose,
what you gain,

when what you always
walk away with -
is *you*.

Below the fear,
in-between breaths,
in forgotten places,
lives a woman
who is capable of it all,

and right now,
she just can't see
how able she really is

because she's weighing
her worth against
her beauty
and not her scars.

RECOVERY IS A HOUSE
you build within yourself.

Each brick a practice
that goes towards creating
a safe space within you.

Each weight-bearing beam
a vital resilience that helps
you mourn your losses.

Each floorboard
a grounding
for your body to rest upon.

And even when
the bricks begin to fall,
when you feel no progress
at all, when the night's long
haul leaves you holding on
to but a few shattered nails,

a ruin is still a holding place.

WE ARE NOT CAPAPBLE
of attaining the light -
of grasping tight
the beauty and wonder
of all that is Love.

But we are able
to shake off the ash -
and allow night's shade
to slip from our shoulders,
revealing the glow
that's already within us.

We are not just a surface
for light to play upon.

We are the waking suns
and burning stars themselves.

HOW DO YOU KNOW
if you are surrendering
or if you are giving up?

There's still space when you surrender,
whereas it's almost like you cannot breathe
when you give up.

Giving up is form of
protecting yourself from the rejection
of what you really want,
so the idea of letting go becomes
very black and white, very now or never.

Surrender is allowing yourself
a little space between you and
the person, place or dream
you've been waiting for, so that you
can see that it's not about
what you want
but more about *the way*
you've been wanting it.

Surrender plants you deeper.
Giving up uproots you.

Surrender holds you.
Giving up pulls the earth
from beneath you.

Surrender is the willing collaboration
with what the great and loving Her
brought you here for.

Giving up is the refusal to believe
that any other plan, person or place
could be better for you than what
your mind has determined alone.

Surrender is the trusting unfolding
of each petal, whereas giving up
is the tight bud that never blooms
because it cannot trust the season.

Giving up hurts us by making us believe
we will never have our goodness, whereas
surrender mends the heart by showing us
all the goodness we already have.

Giving up submissively grieves life's losses.
Surrender actively mourns and moves on.

Surrender gives us time
and most importantly,

rest

from what we've been trying to manifest,
so that we may see what part of us
is still in need of healing,
what part of us is still in need
of growing, what part of us
is still in need of time

before what we long for most
comes to us in its wholeness.

WHEN I WAS LOOKING FOR LOVE
but had none for myself,
I called all things that rejected me, 'love'.

When I was looking for a home
but had none within myself,
I called all kinds of deserts, 'home'.

When I was looking for belonging
but had no sense of it within myself,
I belonged to people who left me,
and the loneliest of places.

When I was looking for peace
but had none within myself,
I could only find a sense of calm
in perfectly still places.

This is how the world outside of us
can appear to fill us - and yet,
leaves our minds, body's and souls
so, so empty.

IT IS COMMON TO BELIEVE
that the more we know,
the more we will know
how to be us.

Pouring information into ourselves
as if we were uncovered wells
feels like we are forever
making wishes
and losing our gold.

Leave spaces for
not knowing.

Allow something to
fill you from
the inside out.

What might bubble up
from deep within you,
like an underground river
finding its way through
those surface cracks
we so often call
boredom, rest, or aloneness?

We will never know ourselves
if we keep telling ourselves
that water is outside of us,
saved for great oceans,
sky gods,
and tree mosses,

only to be poured by others,
only to be given when asked;
our own knowing made lesser
for its quietness
and its work.

Give yourself permission to
softly, tenderly, aimlessly
know yourself

without the noise -

and you will
never find yourself
empty of answers.

RAVEN COMES
when all is vulnerable and open,
when what's left of you
is unprotected and has
nowhere else to hide.

She comes and clears away
what is unusable and futile
to the soul.

She takes away the unwanted,
cleans up after a death
and gathers what's left,
what's sparkly and still beautiful,
to weave into her nest.

Parts of our psyche may seem
fearfully dark at times.

It might feel like Raven,
with her shaggy throat feathers
and Bowie knife of a beak
has found prey in you.

But she knows as you do,

when a death needs to be cleared,
when something inside of you
has rotten away and no longer
provides you with nourishment.

So allow passion and her black wings
to descend upon you,
allow fierce determination
and her golden eyes
to perch upon your shoulder,
allow things to be cleansed
in a way that only the most fearless
part of you knows how.

She is part of the new,
a part of what's to come from this,
through this, because of this...

And She knows as you do,
that you cannot survive
on the bones of an old life,
of an old dream, of an old belief,
of an old relationship that
has lost its meat.

WHO AM I?
It is not only a question
you must ask yourself
when you are alone
under the night lamp
and shadows make
soft silhouettes
upon the blank page.

It is a question to be asked
when there is no light at all
and all you have is a blackened
inner world, to which you must
feel your way through,
from the inside out.

It is a question to be asked
when there is but a glaring sun
cast upon your face and you have
nowhere to hide; your skin,
a narrow barrier of cells and space
that shelter your deep inner world
from the thin outside one.

It is a question to be asked
among plant folk and fish folk
and folk folk...

It is a question and
an answer-to-the-question
of what it means to be whole
and in relationship with the world.

And when you simply
cannot fathom the answer,
you must turn towards
who you are not,

for that is too
a deep and wise knowing.

AS A WOMAN RETURNS
to herself,

so do trees return to the forest
and rivers restore their curves,

so does the fire rise a little higher
and the pot begins to simmer,

so does the smoke begin to curl
and the circle begins to close,

so do the rains return
and the wildflowers bloom,

so does the monarch take flight
and the wolves come home.

YOU CAN STILL FEEL
without being controlled
by that feeling.

You can still love
without being controlled
by that love.

You can still be free
without being controlled
by that freedom.

The most important
empowerment of all
is to simply be with it all

without giving control
to that which makes you feel.

THE BEST VERSION OF ME
is not a different person.

She's not someone who's finally got her shit together. She's not growing her food or composting. She's not making her own tiles or planting mushrooms in her coffee grounds.

She hasn't found her forever home nor does she know what her sole purpose for being here really is. She hasn't mastered the art of timing her body's cycle, creative moods, and need for rest according to the moon's phases. She hasn't figured out how to support herself and her family by working solely on her passion. She's not besties with social media, nor is she an ambassador fighting at the woke-frontlines. She hasn't figured out how to be a functioning highly sensitive mother yet.

She's not a walking boundary-creator. She still doesn't believe there's nothing wrong with her. She's not publicly vulnerable; unfolding her scars bravely to the world. She hasn't become less scared of loss, or love. Her chakras are not in prismatic harmony. She's only 100% plant-based sometimes. She's not confident that every choice is the right one, nor can she always tell the difference between her heart and her mind. She's not become the perfect space holder for others. She doesn't always give herself permission to be herself. She doesn't revive her soul in sweat tents, nor does she have a shaman. She doesn't own a Japanese ceremonial teapot, although she's always looking for the perfect one. She hasn't mastered Zen meditation, nor can she take an 'after photo' yet of her yogic evolution. She's not beyond her circumstances. She hasn't fully surrendered to what she can't control. She is yet to build her creative cabin deep in the redwoods.

She's not become an avid morning person, waking up at 5 am to shape her dreams and reflect on her vision board. She hasn't figured out how to keep all her houseplants alive. She's not a regular blood donor, nor a heart one - although she has given the latter away a few too many times.

The best version of me is not a different person - or an upgrade. The best version of me is someone who decides to stay with me - with that version of me as I already am:

the mess of me, the fragile of me, the scared of me, the trying of me, the traumatized of me, the doubting of me, the grieving of me, the comparing of me, the longing of me, the persistently seeking of me...

She is the version of me who stays and allows the *all of me* to be seen and heard, even when another part of me longs to fix her.

And from this loving and allowing space - all change is possible.

I HAVE LEFT MY GRATITUDES
on the bottom of sea beds,
in the knots of split pine,
in the wooden petals of hemlocks,
and under bridges where worlds meet.

I have shouted them out aloud
across isolated planes,
and whispered them into
crowded rooms.

I have made every footstep a prayer,
every meeting a bow of worship,
every plea an invocation,
every tear an offering.

So, if I ever lose my way,
I will know the way home
by that which was appreciated.

WE HEAR SO OFTEN
the heroine's journey,
from nothing to something,

from quiet to raucous,
from the silent little girl,
to the woman
who found her voice,

from the shy little mouse
she used to be,
to the fierce lioness
she became.

We hear so often the story
of a woman who
found her wild,
became untamed,
who undammed herself,
and then flooded the world.

But what about the other story
of equal value,
the one just as fierce
but half as loud?

The one from *too much*
to just enough -
the one where she goes
on a journey to become
slower and more still,
only to return home
having fought
the inner beasts
of anger, self-fixing,
control and power...

The story of a woman who went
from a *big someone*
to a humble no one,
where she returned softer
more tender, and gentler
around the edges.

The gain and gathering
is what matters
after such journeys -
not what it looks like.

Because sometimes the creatures
within us are not slayed with knives

but with kindness -
and maybe our
thundering homecoming
is actually our quiet leaving,
for good.

And what is sometimes
more fierce and more heroic
than freeing our cry
is our willingness to
listen and be patient.

And when we come out
of the ashes, we are not
flaming birds
but humble cups
that can hold it all.

ALLOW YOURSELF TO BE
absorbed by Love
like a needle resting
on the top of the water,
your sharpness cushioned
by the soft dimple
of what is able to
hug you even at
your most barbed.

THERE IS NO PART OF NATURE
that gives up on itself.

No plant that resigns itself
to the conditions of its hardship,
nor the impossibilities it must face.

Nothing in nature diverts from its purpose;
to fully and unapologetically bloom...

Nor does it want to extract that painful seed
from deep within itself that longs its expansion
because that is exactly what it uses
to grow outward even more.

There's nothing out there in the wild
that does not swell and sprout into what
the Her has asked of it.

No green-bodied being sees the shade
as something against it, as a thief of its light,
but grows *through it*, stretching towards
the sunbeam cast upon the floor.

Patiently, nature always extends itself

beyond what restrains it
by deepening its roots,
and taking up more space...
not less,

never less.

The only difference between us is
that we want control over our conditions,
we want ownership of the sun,
and in that small desire we lose the big truth;
that everything in life comes with a shadow
that we must bend beyond.

Because that's what shadows do -
they make us apprentices of the light,
and you are no less capable of growth,
no less Nature, no less guided,
no less intuitive than that of your kin.

Use the shadows.
Trust the seed.
And if you do collapse as you
journey beyond the darkness,
do it determinedly outward.

YOU DON'T NEED TO FIND
the reason.

You don't need to dive
into the depths of your soul
to find out why you are so anxious,
why you feel so sad, or why
this all feels so hopeless.

You don't need to find the reason.

Stop the excavation,
and leave the bones.

Stop digging up the black well
and give rest to the graves
of others' lost wishes.

Spare the spade, the rake, and hoe
and leave the garden to her weeds.

You don't have to find the reason.

Because knowing the reason
won't always heal you.

It might just give you another bone yard,
another well, another thick creeper
with its tangled and strangling vines…

Leave the thorns to the wilder garden
and nurture yourself forward.

You will naturally weed ache by
rewilding yourself, and this means
allowing everything within you
to grow in balance with everything else.

The weeds will begin to
mother the butterflies and feed the bees.

Your dandelions and daises
will begin to offer you medicine
and their unassuming beauty
might just leave you awe-struck one day.

Make your beauty taller.
Make your wholeness thicker.
Give your worthiness taproots.

Make the extensions of your Heart -

those silently stretching limbs of yours
bend towards the light.

You don't always have to root out
the reason for your longing, for your ache,
for why this moment isn't enough -
but foster the growth of greater goodness,
allowing the extending canopy of presence
to cast itself over all.

Everything else will naturally fall into the
undergrowth, enriching the mulch
to which true healing grows.

BEING WITH YOUR ALONENESS
is never being alone.

It's a dance
with everything that's
reaching forward to touch you,
to help you remember your
undeniable company.

The air hugging your skin,
the candlelight arching towards you,
the pots of flowers beaming their best
just to be noticed by you,
the water asking to be a part of you,
the singing birds serenading you,
the cold feet asking for
the friendship of socks...

being truly alone is
being comfortable enough
to be met by friends who live
just beneath the ache of silence.

MAYBE I DON'T NEED TO CONSIDER
the worthiness of my work today.

Maybe that internal debate can be
put in a jar and set high upon a shelf,
and left to wither a little
along with other things
I've been meaning to question.

Maybe dust can collect upon
that pondering, and maybe it can
just sit there, seeping in its own
limbo juices...

Until I have one of those
strong moments,
you know, one of those
just-had-a-cold-swim,
just-felt-deep-gratitude,
just-created-a-little-space,
kind of moments...

and I feel like I'm in a good place,
like nothing can shake me -

and only then will I pull down
that consideration and place it
on the table, and blow dust off it,
and shake it a little to either side,
and look closely at that
shriveled up question
in all its triviality and stagnancy
and probably do
what I do with all things
that have become stale...

Yes, I'd rather do that
than question it now
when its juicy and raw,
and its impact could soak
the rest of my day in bitterness.

It's from which mind state we face our pain
that matters most to our healing, dear beloved.

I AM TEACHING MY BODY
to be in a new way, for it has
only ever known conflict and
shame, struggle and, pain.

And this means opening myself up
so that I can feel something else,
something quite new and
never experienced before.

I know fear will creep in and tell me
that what I'm doing is wrong, or not enough,
or too much or just pointless - but that's just what
fear does, it justifies itself by invalidating Love.

And I won't resist those feelings,
(because that's what fear loves most)
I will just tenderly and curiously allow
it all to be, and then let what hurts
pass without judgment, without the need
to fix or change anything.

Because I know healing can be uncomfortable -
not because the medicine is terribly sour
but because the body has to get used

to something else.

The body is suddenly being asked to be ok
with contentment and ease, and needs to
make a little more space for joy and excitement.

And this might feel foreign at first -
but not as foreign as I've felt
inside of my own skin for so many years.

I'm willing to feel it all now, to allow it all
to pass through me, without resistance
but with the commitment to keep moving
forward, shedding one piece
of that ache at a time...

knowing that this threshold -
between the old and the new,
between the past and the future,
between the story and the next blank page -
marks the place of my return.

WE ALL BELIEVE
that in order for something
to be true,
it must be complex.

But the deepest,
most powerful and
life-changing truths
are essentially
very simple.

You must allow the Heart
to boil things down for you.

Let Her make you potent
so nothing but
the plainness of breath,
the basicness of quiet,
and the clarity of presence
profoundly heals you.

SOMETIMES
the fiercest forgiveness
we can offer ourselves
is between the woman
we had to become
in order to survive

and who we could been
without her.

DESERT WOMEN
parched, bleached, cleaned,
pressed down, preserved…

Arid, scorched, thirsty,
always thirsty,
we know these women;
like oil paper and dry sponges.

So happens to be
the epitome of attraction
and yet attraction itself is
made up of primordial dew,
the flowing rapture of
dirt and salt and water,
of silk and steam.

Water women,
moist, mist, saturated, soaked,
the cloth that captures the rain,
the porous earth that feeds the roots.

Let the floodwaters meet you,
and make you an oasis
in our wasteland of desert women.

MAY ALL THAT COMES YOUR WAY
in life be embraced within a
container of Love.

If it is a depression, a crisis,
a fear, a struggle -
may it exist within
a greater boundary
so that your life becomes
a life of Love -
that happens to be
experiencing pain,
and not a life of pain itself.

May you become that vessel,
and may all be dissolved within
the great ocean of your vastness.

EVERYTHING IMPORTANT BEGINS
the moment you free yourself
from that little lie.

You know the one -
the one that says you're fine,
that you can go on for a little longer,
that you don't really need what you need,
that you can lose that thing you said
you'd never lose but somehow,
because of them, because of time,
because of age… it got lost,
along with other sacred
and precious things.

Free the little lie, you know the one -
the one that's right here,
bursting from your bitten lip,
rippling away from your
tightened body in small waves of silence.

Say it, write it, wring it from your bones,
sing it from your heart, this is my little lie:

_____

..........and then you will be free.

But remember, beautiful and brave soul,
that this freedom will feel like
a very fearsome place to be at first.

It will feel like surviving the
Northern tundra with little knowledge
of how to light your own fire
or find your own way in the dark.

But you will be free
and the stars will know it,
the moon will know it,
and the beasts will begin
to recognize you as their own...

and then you will come
to know yourself among
the true and wild things in this life,

which is where
you have always belonged.

SOMETIMES HAPPINESS
is so foreign to us that
even when we have it,
we feel a sense of wrongness
about having it.

And so we find ways,
even meaningful ways,
even honorable ways
of going back to
the suffering we know.

We invite old longings back
and conflicts to stay
and the fixing of others
to take up all our energy.

We are healed and whole
- but because it's unfamiliar -
we would rather go back
to our sense of certainty.

Healing is allowing yourself
to be happy, it is to allow yourself
to reside within an unfamiliar truth.

FROM THE ONLY ANGLE
we can see,
the thin web looks
fragile and frail.

But not from
Spider's point of view.

She's always
hauling course yarn,
hitching lines and looping
braided ropes around the
best possible posts.

It's tiresome work,
fighting slack,
winching up the give,
starting over
and over again…

It isn't ever
delicate work
to live.

SOME MAY NOTICE
your quietness and call it
a taming - but *softening* may be
the wildest act of all.

Wild is not a sound,
it is not something that
can be seen or heard by others.

It's a personal journey,
a way of walking
and only the tracks
you leave behind
garnish the true scent
of your soul.

Your journey is your own,
no one can tell you how to
walk it, heal it, grow it -
and whatever it takes
to claim ownership
of your personal path
is what makes you truly wild,

be that a roar or a quiet receding.

ALL OF THIS
everything you are doing
right now

is a reclamation
of your right to be here,

just as you are.

IT'S IN THE LISTENING
that we remember.

So, bow down to the
kings and queens
of silence, to the
sovereign voices
of the undergrowth,

for the Elder's wisdom
wasn't passed down
through word but
through water and seed.

Silence speaks to the
foot's bare sole
and the body's curve
as we are ushered to rest.

Those ways to live better were
tucked into the trumpet vine,
the sweet pepperbush,
the wild potatoes flower,
and the ripe and plump
inky black bulb of blackberry.

And as the desert quietly moans
under the weight of dune,
and the underwater heartbeat
thuds against the scales of fish,

and as the tide reach toward moon,
and sun drips his tears
through the canopy,
and the eyelid opens as bear
awakens in spring,

voices rise from the ground
like ochre dust.

All is speaking to us,
let us listen,
let us listen.

LOVE IS NO TEMPLE
no shrine to worship,
no confession room.

It is a miracle and you do not
need to worship it from afar
but hold it like a vibrant bloom,
allowing everything to
constantly fall apart
so it can come back
together again more whole.

Love is no church, but the
fruit-bearing tree that flourishes
on the graveyard's ground.

They try to sanction the sacred,
put it inside of things,
into practices and certain places

but everything is already
inside the sacred
and cannot be removed.

SHOOK FROM THE TREE
you are loosened from yourself
and you fall to the ground.

The cycle of pain and healing
seem so separate at times
but it is the same hand
that causes you to fall
as the one that allows you
to grow.

Healing and shedding are part
of the same seed.

And how you fall - how you respond
to the gravity that pulls you away
from what you know;
whether you curse the sky
or honor the ground -
is up to you.

That is what little-but-mighty
power you have in this life,
dear beloved.

LIFE HAS A WAY OF MAKING
women become one of two things;
some become protectors,
war maidens, slayers of
anything that might steal away
their few precious things.

These stone-women believe
every situation, place, or person
is a carver; a knife-wielding shaper
who wants to change her...

the job she hates, the partner she regrets,
the places she has no say in staying in -
they all slice deep rivets into her
making her into someone she must protect
at all costs, for she has little control
over anything else.

But some women become
their own sculptor and keep
themselves soft so she can use
every situation, place, and person
to tenderize her into
whom she decides to be.

These artists know
that they have a choice in
who holds the knife,
even when at times,
that choice is the hardest
thing to accept.

Hardness is often a sign
of a dream that went missing,
or something vital that lost its way
in its own becoming.

Somewhere along the line
choice was taken out of
stone-woman's hands and placed
inside another's, and in her innocence,
she mistook her Maker for someone
she needed to prove herself to,
to mark herself for,
and give herself up
in order to please.

Harder, more closed, unrecognizable
war maidens become to the soul;
their straightness makes them like arrows,

so sharp, they never stop
going through whatever they meet.

It is the artist who allows the soul
to flow through her like a river -
she bends to the greater hand that
sustains her journey with sway and
oxbows, so she rests along
life's long body.

If you, like I, have become hardened
there is always a way back
to the gentleness that cushions,
nourishes and therefore
fertilizes new life…

Softness is not the result of a
soul-driven life, dear beloved,
but the only way back into it.

Don't wait for things to be easier
in order for you to be softer -
choose tenderness as a way of living
in order to return home to yourself.

I CAN FEEL THE ANGER
without the fear of anger.

I can feel the despair
without the fear of despair.

I can feel the anxiety
without the fear of anxiety.

I can feel the disconnect
without the fear of disconnect.

Because struggle is not caused
by how I feel…
but by the fear I place around it.

Emotions, without the
dry kindling of fear,
are just emotions
that never become bonfires.

IT IS KNOWN THAT
the closer you get to what
you really want,
the more you will encounter
your split...

that is because your spilt
always lies on the threshold
between your dream
and its manifestation.

Your split always makes itself known
just as you are about to walk
through that door, and asks you
to face that thing that you
do not wish to face.

And so, you may come close
to what you desire most many times
but always walk away from that door;
that invitation to heal the unhealed.

Perhaps this time though, this dream
will bring you close enough once more,
and perhaps you will face that thing

that has been waiting for you -
on the threshold of the mundane
and the magical.

And perhaps life will never be the same
because a dream being lived
is the sign of a wound
being healed.

All wild wanderings take us
to the most exciting places,
so bravery is what counts most
on the path of our dreams,
not because dreams are difficult
to make real but because *we*
are what we always find
standing in the way of them.

Embodying a dream and healing
are really one of the same, dear beloved.

LOVE, LEAVE BEHIND
the mental health story
written by others
who saw your sensitivity
as a weakness and your
empathy as an inconvenience.

Leave behind those
who never took the time
to understand you
because they were knee-deep
in their own struggles.

Many have fallen before you,
not because they were broken
but because they were
misunderstood,
misdiagnosed,
and misjudged.

Don't let others' careless words
fall upon your page,
it's your page, your book,
your life, your choice.

The most important task
you will ever have
is to take the time you need
to understand yourself
and your story.

What part of it
have you made into a life?

What parts of yourself have
you had to lose in order
to live this story?

All is regained
by grabbing the pen
between your fingers
with the willingness to know
who you could be
if written by your
innate wholeness instead.

SUFFERING DOESN'T
always mean healing.

At some point you
have to choose joy
in order to move on.

WHEN WE ARE VISIBLE
we can be seen,
and when we can be seen
we can be touched,
and when we are touched
we can be hurt.

All of us create
elaborate ways of
looking like we are
showing up
without the work of
showing up.

We are all struggling to be here
in our bodies, in our minds
against life's fierce need
to change us.

HOW CAN YOU SEE
the magic when all you see is
the mediocre, the hurt,
the struggle?

But if pain is all you see,
then how can you
possibly see anything else?

And while you tremble,
and the earth dislodges
your foundations,

remember these pieces
that you think you are losing
are in fact an unburdening.

Can you allow the earth
to fall away from beneath
your feet and trust the
gentle undercurrent that
carries you to freedom?

TRAUMA OFTEN PUSHES US
away from others, just so we can
separate ourselves from more hurt.

But sometimes there is no wound
beneath the pull that wants us
to be alone in vast, expansive places.

In fact, it is not *disconnect* that calls us
to seek out these solitary places, but a
deep yearning to reunite with ourselves.

What we need to become aware of
is whether we are pushing ourselves
away from others
or
being pulled towards
our wild aloneness.

I DIDN'T FALL IN LOVE WITH HER
on an island or in wild mountains,
or in the lush forests of tropical lands.

I fell in love with Her here in the flatlands
and the farmlands, where the cold bodies
of water helped me feel again.

I didn't need Her while I was
in places that needed nothing from me -
I needed Her when everything had been
bitten off me and I had become
moth-ridden with nothing left to give.

I found my freedom, not with bare feet
but with an unguarded heart that allowed
me to sink into its unfamiliar warmth
while winter crept into the dark corners
of this lonely house.

Changes were made from cemetery benches
and damp tents on frozen mornings where
discomfort poured the coffee
and exhaustion served the oats,
and nothing but breathing made sense.

I wanted the sun and her flowers,
and the open wild fields to carry me back
to myself, but I had none, so carried myself
and fell in love with what was there
under those forlorn Northern skies.

We find our strengths in
strange moments, away from the idyllic
ideas and places we dream for ourselves.

SHE IS QUIET
as she wades through
the grass of hip-high barley,

taking her time to
split the long silky stems
with her nail and flick seeds
across the field.

She is soft in her wanting
and strong in her surrender,
knowing there is time for her
to be it all
and for all
to become her.

Nothing ever comes untimely,
she knows.

Nothing good exists without her
being a part of it.

Nothing ever comes too much
or too little, everything is just
as it should be, always helping

her remember, always
helping her grow.

Everything offers itself
over and over to her,
falling gently at her feet
for the creation of more joy.

Nothing sacred passes her by,
it's all here...

she just needs to see it,
and through her allowing
of unconditional worthiness -

she takes what she needs,
leaving the rest
to feed the earth.

YES, I REMEMBER WHAT I AM

I remember through the deep inner call that unravels me at the sight of new snow, the smell of the leaves pooled in the hollow of a trunk. I remember it all when my nose sinks into a jar of cardamom or when my fingertips become stained with turmeric. I remember when I bite into the leaf of a cinnamon tree and when I touch the satiny ash of freshly burnt sage.

I am called back to myself through those moments of courage when my skin becomes electric from cold water. I know my place when my hand runs over the ancient ripples of red rock.

I remember how to live well, with meaning and purpose, guided by my own star, my own constellation, weaving my body and its own beliefs together with the cosmos. I remember how to call in my tribe, I remember Circle and hands and the smell of juniper cast on an open fire.

I remember wildflowers and nettles and the help of Moon lighting up the path home after a long night. I remember the midnight sun, sleeping in my skin listening to when it needed rest and it needed movement.

I remember the intoxication of love, freedom, creativity, and autonomy; to be as I pleased, to be myself.

Also the pain, I remember the pain that became a teacher. I remember the broken body in recovery, my broken mind in rehabilitation, slowly mending the delicate threads that kept me intact. I remember the trust it required and the rest it demanded. I remember my willingness to give away all my control just to feel the ease of being supported.

I remember, mostly in my forgetting. The moment I blame, shame, and hurry. I remember that this is not the truth and if I come back to Love, I come back to who I really am.

Yes, I remember what it means to be whole.

I CHOOSE THE LIGHT
by not fearing the dark,
by offering my presence
to the full spectrum of
my emotions.

I do not vilify nor glorify
certain states of being.

I allow all to exist
within the
limitless container
that is me,
that is Love.

a mantra

I NO LONGER DROWN IN DREAMS
there are now small pockets of air
in my lungs where I can take a few
short breaths and survive...

and when I plummet into the watery bed,
or when my loved ones sink
like heavy rocks all the way down
into the dark deep,
I am now able to invoke the
webbed feet and slit gills
of an amphibian that allows me
to fiercely swim back up
to the surface.

I'm not afraid of drowning anymore
nor of being helpless and victimized
by my life, my thoughts, and my emotions.

I decide what survives now
because I have an aqualung.

NEVER FORGET THE MEAT
and the marrow
of who you are.

without the flesh, there is no spirit,
without the roots, there is no tree,
without the substance and the soil,
nothing can grow.

The mess and the human
are part of the sacred and the divine;
they are one of the same.

And when you commune
with the sacred,
never forget it is the
hand, the knees, the belly
the lungs, the spongy mind matter
that speaks and it is
the Heart that listens.

Moon lulling tide,
kissing the ebb.

TIME TO GRIEVE

we must have time to grieve,
we must make space to grieve,
for there is much that has been lost.

And sometimes what is
most bereaved
is not what came to be
but what never came at all.

For it is our unlived lives
that hurt us the most.

I NO LONGER DROWN IN DREAMS
there are now a small pockets of air
in my lungs where I can take a few
short breaths and survive...

and when I plummet into the watery bed,
or when my loved ones sink
like heavy rocks all the way down
into the dark deep,
I am now able to invoke the
webbed feet of an amphibian
and the slit gills that allow me
to fiercely swim back up
to the surface.

I'm not afraid of drowning anymore
nor of being helpless and victimized
by my life, my thoughts, and my emotions.

I decide what survives now.

I decide what gets to live inside of me.

FORGIVENESS MEANS SIMPLY
opening the door to your heart again
and being prepared
to abandon all hope,
once and for all,
that the past could have
been any different.

The past is here to help you
come closer to your heart,
and when you reconcile
and grieve fully
into the seams of your body
for what has gone
and what never came to be -

you forgive everything.

NO ONE BELONGS HERE
We are all birthed from myth,
from the soft fur that shawls
the curve of reindeer ear,

from the ebony beak of Raven who
fastened the earth into place,
from forbidden gardens and
the rib of loneliness,

from women who fell through
sky and Turtle's back,
from Lotus flower,

sprung from the navel of deity,
from the flesh of battling brothers,
we drink from the rivers of their blood,
and live upon the mountain of their bones,

from curled-up scale
of sleeping Rainbow Serpent,
from Cosmic Golden Egg,
and moonblood…

We are all vagabonds

living in a world that
was created not only
before us, but *for* us.

We are custodians.
We are this earth's conscious travelers,
not its origin, nor its maker.
And those who came before us
still watch over their creation.

They are the ones who
still live in the forests,
who still watch with eyes hung
from the moon cloth of
midnight body.

No one belongs here really,
we are all stewards of mystery,
and our true home,
our origin beyond culture,
nation and country,
is not of this world.

And 'to belong'
is to find that

balance between the *being*
and the *longing* -
to return to the nest of canopy
as well as root ourselves in
the substance of soil.

Remember this when you feel
that inexplicable ache
to return 'home'
when you feel
no place, person, or country
could possibly
hold the shape of you.

You are child of
Sun and Sky,
you are life's rapturous
desire to exist,
and bear witness to
what marvels grew
while you slumbered
for eons as a seed of the cosmos.

Consciousness is the gift of home
just as life is the gift of mystery.

MAY WE ALWAYS REMEMEBR
that there is a secret bond
between slow
and remembering

and hurry
and forgetting.

THERE LIES A STRETCH OF TIME
between who you are now
and whom you are becoming.

She stands just ahead of you
and the only difference
is her lived experience.

She knows something
you are yet to,
just as you know something
that woman in your past
is yet to.

So the truth is that
you are always
embodying a wisdom
that is useful
to your situation right now.

Because if you keep telling
your inexperienced self
how to make it through,
so too will the woman
just in front of you

get her message back to you.

And this unconditional wisdom
rarely changes in advice and tone.

Just as you would tell
your younger self
to keep going,
that it's going to be ok,
that you must keep
returning to yourself...

so too is your timeless self
speaking through black holes
that same message back to you.

I AM ON A MISSION TO RECLAIM
that small child inside of me
that used to run barefoot and conquer
trees with effortless joy and ease.

I'm on a mission to discover
what made me abandon her
in the pressure to be grown
and fully bloomed -

when the real beauty was in
slowing down enough to watch
her find her roots and sprout
her bright green leaves.

I somehow got caught up in a world
that didn't think innocence
was sacred or that curiosity
was a way of life.

A world that put significance
on numbers and bestowed gifts to
those who sat still - who gave out
golden stars to those who agreed,
and applauded those who thought laterally.

I was given the idea
that by being wholly me,
I would never succeed.

It was a world that stole away
my preciousness and then taught me
to seek my whole life for
what's precious outside of me.

A thief of a world
that kept taking my valuables
and then selling me back
what was already mine.

I'm on a mission to feed that child
everything she needs to grow healthy
and strong, and give echo to her voice
that sings her soul home,

because she is the only one
who truly knows Love;
how to make it an offering,
but most importantly,
how to make it a receiving.

I'm on a mission to free the girl within
that thought everything was a miracle
and anything was possible,
even when it was not...

I still want to climb that hill -
the one that doesn't reward me
for reaching the top
but the one that lines foothills
and caves with kindred hearts
who offer me hot tea and a seat
at the fireside, before I brave
the next ascent.

I'm on a mission to give her the keys
to my life and for her to drive it
wherever her heart pleases.

And maybe my mission is not really
a mission but a gentle letting go,
because I know she never left me
and is always here.

I don't want to wait until I'm so frail
that my inner youth has the power

to overthrow me and strip me of my cares,
for the old and the young are
as thick as thieves and as free as birds.

I want her to walk with me
the whole way, the middle-life
being her revival and reclamation
of that sacred child
who got lost long ago.

FEMININITY IS NOT
a plumpness of skin
nor the flick of full hair,
it is not the scent of lavender,
nor the degree of curve
just above the hip...

It is the way you carry yourself
through some of the hardest
moments of your life.

It is the humble bowing down
and praying at the soft feet of
your own grace.

It is the mothering of
your own flesh
as it defies your will.

Feminity is fertility and war,
and as all deities know,
the hand that gives
is the one that takes too.

Femininity does not always choose

the dove's feather when She knows
that the raven black plume is
more necessary to carry you forwards.

She knows what to give
and to whom,
and it is never more
than She knows you can bear.

Femininity is a fierceness;
a determination to not hide
but to bravely be seen...
and not in spite of
the discomfort -
but because of it.

What makes you feel fragile
on the outside is an invitation
from Her to grow in inner strength.

THE THING ABOUT PAIN STORIES
is that they don't tend to change.

We change, our bodies change,
our wrinkles ripple outward like
small pebbles cast from our eyes,
our skin begins to migrate south
and hugs the earth, we finally meet
with what we have perched ourselves
above for so long, our Heart moves on,
pulling us towards, *always towards*
the whole and the hopeful...

but the pain story says the same;
the story of hurt and trauma stays airless,
lifeless, stagnant; a hidden pool within us
where all our lost things live, where all
which came in a pair become singular
and useless.

And when we truly want to move on,
our story lets us know that
it is truly impossible.

And when we want to

wholeheartedly love again,
our protective story pulls us aside
and reminds us that it's far too painful.

And when we want to heal,
our broken story masks itself
as a healer and takes us into her arms
promising to comfort us, vowing to fix us,
praying we will not discover that it is
her that is in need of healing.

It's ok, dear beloved because our stories
are just doing what all stories do
in order to survive -
they perpetually rewrite themselves
into existence using any material
we give them that validates their continuation.

For the death of a story is scary,
not to the core you, but to the mind
because it finds comfort
in what's predictable, rehearsed, and known.

So the mind depends on you becoming less
so it can fit itself into you.

But the Heart? It's not so sticky,
it's not so high maintenance
nor does it require the indigo of ink
to be seen and heard.

It validates itself by loving more,
by opening more, by forgiving more.

The Heart lives in between the story's words,
along the ridge of the book's spine,
it is the paper itself, the stitches and folds,
the beginning and end, the blank page
before pen, and the writer herself.

And the Heart asks that you
become *more*
so you can fit into it.

IT IS ALWAYS AT THE HOUR
of uncertainty that we pick the flowers,
that we take the silver teaspoon
from the drawer, that we wash
ourselves with herbs and oils,
that we dress and garland ourselves
in a way most suited to our souls,
and comb our hair ready for
our maker.

Why not the rest of our days,
for the honor we have
been given in life?

I HAVE AN UNFETTERED SPIRIT
and always will.

I long for wide, open
and untouched places, and
sometimes this yearning
calls me beyond the hedge,
beyond the smallness of
my everyday life.

It feels like I mistakenly left my skin
out at sea and it got swallowed up
by the tide, and I forever come across
this scent of embodiment, only to always
come short of its union.

My kin of scale, feather and fur
know me by my Heart and they
wonder why I'm still here...
why I keep these two feet,
why I don't just get on with it
and grow out my tail already.

I know my daughter will too
feel this chasmal echo within her,

and so will hers, and we will all
concern ourselves with questions
of how to live in between that
insatiable longing to return to the moon -
and the necessity of being fully present
with our earthly tide.

I will show her that there is a fine veil
that separates us from
another world full of magic,
but that she needs to be here,
really here, in order to see it,
because it's not somewhere else,
and never will be -
it's all *from* her,
it's all within.

And when she comes across the scent
of her soul's home, I will remind her
never to get lost in trying to return to it,

because lives lived
only from longing,
are no lives lived at all.

SHE, WHO DECLARES
to have reclaimed herself
only to come back to the surface
with little but a handful of soil -
knows little about what
true reclamation is.

The word reclamation means
"to call the hawk back to the glove"
to call back the spirit to the body,
to call back the heart to the life...

and to call back is no meek cry
in the direction of what's gone missing
but the bottomless roar
of the birthing mother
who calls her body back
from the primordial gateway.

Reclamation is the ultimate
heroine's journey where sometimes
we lose our limbs
just to gain perspective.

And once we have the

still-beating heart in our hands,
the molten core burning through
the delicate pads of our palms…

once we have grown gills
and have mapped the floor beds
of a thousand seas and her shipwrecks,
once we bear the scars of multiple descents
all over our body,

…then we can say that we've
reclaimed what went missing
through the disembodiment of trauma.

IN LONELINESS, I ASKED THE PAST
to bring me all the women whose blood
runs through my veins…

and they came,
and they sat beside me,
and they listened.

I recognized a few of whom I'd met,
and remembered their toughness;
how life had shaped them with
wire brushes and caustic soda.

And I considered what softness
they could offer me when they themselves
weren't given the privileges of
lapping words and loving hands.

Some of them had been exiled by
life's hardships and never found
their way home.

Some were numbed by the bluntness
of an unchosen life and simply
couldn't walk away from the

heavy ropes of responsibility.

But then I realized that
I did not need whom life made them into
but who they were in spite of that,
who they were under that,
who they were through that.

I needed their hearts, untrodden,
and left wild.

Because the wild never dies in any woman
no matter how long it has been
since their pelt was worn,
since their soles were padded and
their spines arched towards Moon.

It was that remembrance that
softened me and all the forgiveness
spilled out and all the love poured in.

And my hands flushed warm
from a hundred women kin
whose palms totem'd upon mine.

And it didn't matter which
foremothers arrived because
because it was only their heart I needed,
it's only the heart we are ever in search of.

THE KEY TO LIFE
is not found in
figuring out all the answers
but in offering yourself
to your questions.

Devote yourself to them,
for they came with you
to this place of blackened soil
and milk-ladled moons.

Unknowns are residues
of the Great Mystery herself
who birthed you into
this world of cloaks and veils,

and knowing it all
would rob us of
your art and the beauty
of all your sense-making.

How you live your questions
is a night lamp for others
to find their own way
in life's eclipsing sun.

GROWING IN YEARS
to many of us,
is a boiling,
a scalding,
a breaking...

whereas,
it is really a steaming -
the kind that softens and
opens and unfurls us

as if we were being asked
to let in heaven
a little more.

LONGINGS ARE LIKE WELLS
so deep they plunder
into our own psyches
that sometimes we catch
the glint of a coin, a relic
from an ancestor past who cast
such a great wish that it went
through the water, which turned
into sky, which flipped the whole
world upside down, and gravity
shifted, and the coin began to fall
from that watery sky down towards
the earth and into that well
that is you.

All we have ever longed for
is to be whole,
is to be home,
is to be here.

That is why we turn into stars
to reflect upon the depth
of our own want.

IN THE END
from all our travels,
from the many dead ends,
and no ends, and never ends,
from the early rises, and high tides,
from the weight and demands,
from the tears and deep breaths...

we are not made into gods
but humbled into grace.

And if we're lucky,
overcoming our struggles
will make us *more* human.

To you, the one who reads these words, who gave this book a place to rest, perhaps even a home...

I will be forever grateful for the space you created within yourself so something new could grow.

Your own words are more powerful than anyone else's, so speak to yourself from the heart and you will always find your way through the darkness.

If you feel this book would be of service to another, please consider giving it away to a friend, or use the power of your voice to review it on Amazon or Goodreads, so that someone in search of healing might find it.

I sincerely thank you for your time in responding to these words in any way you feel called to.

Your sister in Heart,
Sez

Would you like to read more of my poems? Find them on Substack: www.substack.com/sezkristiansen

All the lessons from this book in affirmations

I am capable. I am resilient. I belong. Everything I need is inside of me. I am slow, intentionally. I am wild. I always choose Love over fear. I am learning to be fully myself. I am returning to the curious, vulnerable, and awe-filled girl I used to be. I am re-mothering myself. I am deeply creative. I am gentle and kind. I am primordial dew. I am a channel for Grace to pour itself through. I am allowing a little more Heaven in. I am whole, home and here. I am humble. I am reclaiming myself. I am living my questions. I am forgiving it all. I am of feather and fur too. I am sacred. I am more than my pain story. I can see in the dark. I can breathe underwater. I let go of what no longer provides me with substance. I know who I am. I choose joy. I am embodying my dream. I am not my emotions. I am the greater vessel. I am deeply grateful. I am returning to myself. I am Her.

Made in the USA
Middletown, DE
08 July 2023

34735512R00066